The Digital Learner

Dedications:

To the hardworking Educational Community around the world,
Thank you; Keep on Learning, Teaching, Inspiring!

To the students whose generation transitioned to independent
learning and are now teaching the ins and outs of EdTech
to their teachers; The Students Become the Masters!

To Ansar, my loving husband, who has been my guiding light in this
ever-changing technological world – Thank you for Everything!

To order additional copies of this book, contact:
Xlibris
844-714-8691
www.Xlibris.com
Orders@Xlibris.com

ISBN: Softcover   978-1-6698-3664-3
        Hardcover   979-8-3694-0461-4
        EBook   978-1-6698-3663-6

Print information available on the last page

Rev. date: 07/30/2023

The Digital Learner

A Saved Story from
the Memory of Mr. Time-Bot,
The Class Robot!

A.K. KHAN

Once long ago, in a time when traditional teaching and learning met digital innovation, the classroom became a realm of endless possibilities.

It all began during a very special week in school!

The school was getting brand-new bright-colored computers, shiny laptops, colorful tablets, giant Smart Boards, and joining all this technology was Mr. Time-Bot, the rolling class robot, at your service.

All this was in celebration of Educational Technology Week!

Everyone was excited except one...

ALLY HATED TECHNOLOGY!

Everyone Ally's age had a cell phone or loved to play games on a laptop or did hours of research on a computer.

But *not* Ally...

"It was going to be a digital disaster!", thought Ally, as Mr. Time-Bot observed everyone.

Ally felt useless. Ally did not like change.

How was she going to use these electronic machines!

Ally loved the smell of paper books—not electronic books behind a screen.

Ally loved to write with a flowy smooth pen or freshly sharpened pencil for hours on lined paper, not type on a screen.

How was she going to manage to do all her work with all this new technology?

I'll be the biggest failure ever! Ally thought.

Ally loved her colorful classroom filled with positive energy but all this technology was scaring her.

She promised herself to try to embrace this new change for everyone in the class.

That morning, Ally decided to be brave and use the new computer for Math class.

Guess what? It was a digital disaster!

Ally decided to do some Math problems. First she turned on the Power button, and the computer started. All was well, so far.

Then she clicked a familiar icon and a new window opened. She finally began typing in the new website address, but it didn't work.

Someone began yelling, "No, you're missing an *A*"; another said, "No, you're missing a *T*," and another interjected, "No, you have to double click."

Ally quickly moved back to paper and pencil and finished the Math problems, and soon, so did everyone else.

mathproblems.com

PAGE NOT FOUND!

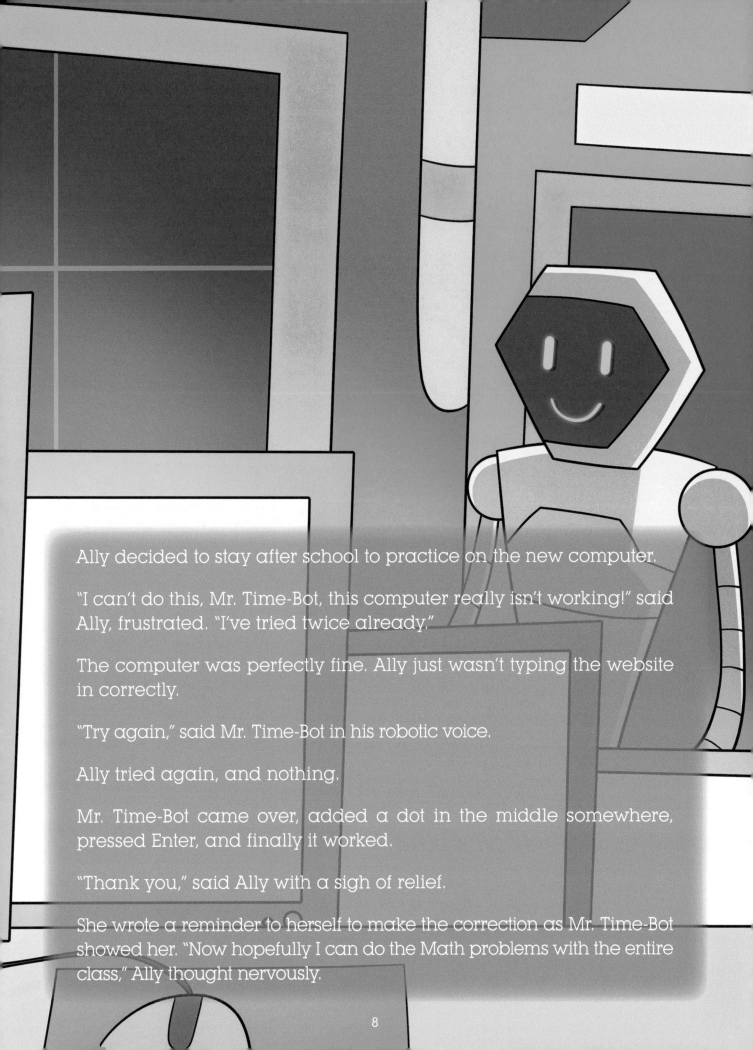

Ally decided to stay after school to practice on the new computer.

"I can't do this, Mr. Time-Bot, this computer really isn't working!" said Ally, frustrated. "I've tried twice already."

The computer was perfectly fine. Ally just wasn't typing the website in correctly.

"Try again," said Mr. Time-Bot in his robotic voice.

Ally tried again, and nothing.

Mr. Time-Bot came over, added a dot in the middle somewhere, pressed Enter, and finally it worked.

"Thank you," said Ally with a sigh of relief.

She wrote a reminder to herself to make the correction as Mr. Time-Bot showed her. "Now hopefully I can do the Math problems with the entire class," Ally thought nervously.

The next day in Math, Ally was so proud of herself. She was able to finally get to the correct website and do the Math problems with the class.

An adventure of learning began as the first keystrokes echoed through the digital classroom.

But when it was time for English…

Guess what? It was a digital disaster!

The rest of the classes were playing a great interactive vocabulary game that many kids were enjoying, but when Ally opened her laptop and started the app, she couldn't understand how to begin. Everyone was staring at her, and they began to help her. "Press the yellow pencil" one person yelled. "It might be the red triangle," said another. "Shut it down and turn it back on again," said someone from the back, but Ally felt embarrassed and decided to move on with her vocabulary words on flashcards and a pen, and soon, so did everyone else.

Later that day, Ally decided to bring her laptop to lunch. She finally mustered the courage to ask her friends for help.

"I'm having trouble figuring out how to play this vocabulary game in English class. I've seen you all playing it in your classes, can one of you please show me?" Ally said hesitantly.

"Sure!" said her friends.

Soon Ally was zooming through the game! "Thank you, I can finally play the game with my English class now," said Ally gratefully.

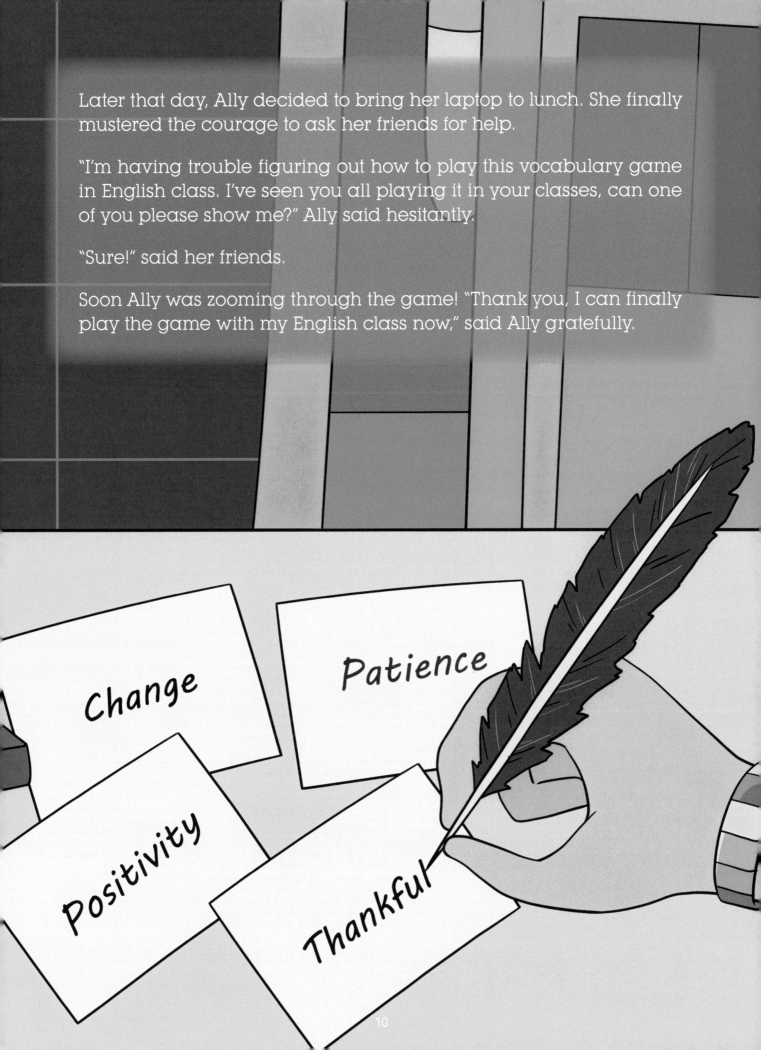

The next day, Math and English were a breeze. Ally was very thankful to get help from her friends and was grateful that she was learning new things. Maybe she was stressing over all this new technology for no reason.

The digital classroom gave life to new possibilities at the beginning of a technological revolution.

But later that afternoon when it was time for Science...

Guess what? It was a digital disaster!

They were going to take a virtual field trip to the Science museum through the Smart Board, which was exactly like a regular board, but it definitely was *not*; it was an interactive computerized board with a giant touch screen, and Ally was unfortunately always in the way of the sensor. The screen was shifting up and down and sideways; it just wouldn't stay still.

The others kept yelling, "Move to the right!" "No, move to the left!" "Duck down!" "Freeze!"

Ally was frustrated! She just went back to her desk and quietly read her Science magazine instead, and soon, so did everyone else.

The blank Smart Board stayed open and blurred into a rainbow of pastel colors, and once class was over, Mr. Time-Bot came to visit and saw the Smart Board on.

"What do we have here?" said Mr. Time-Bot, filled with curiosity.

"The virtual field trip won't work," Ally said sadly.

Mr. Time-Bot went to the Smart Board and clicked on the settings and turned the sensor off. "Now you can project what you like and the screen will stay put," said Mr. Time-Bot, "but if you want to ever write on the Smart Board, then you have to turn the sensor on again."

Ally looked horrified. "Write on this! I'll stick to the old traditional way of writing for now," Ally said, frightened.

"Everything will come to you with practice, all in good time!" said Mr. Time-Bot optimistically. He flashed a smiley face on his face before he rolled away.

The next day, Math, English, and Science were all surprisingly fun. Ally was happy she got some training from Mr. Time-Bot.

It was the dawn of the digital classroom; a world where textbooks met pixels.

But later on when it was time for History

Guess what? It was a digital disaster!

Ally was a nervous wreck again. It was the day to use the class tablets. The class was going to watch an important presidential speech while answering questions on the tablet simultaneously, at the same time.

It sounded easy, but it wasn't. Some of the kids couldn't hear anything, some couldn't find the disappearing keyboard on the tablet, and some were continuously rotating their screen to keep everything from turning sideways.

Ally was frozen; she couldn't do anything. It seemed like everyone was getting confused. So she quickly turned off her tablet and moved on to the History textbook instead, and soon, so did everyone else.

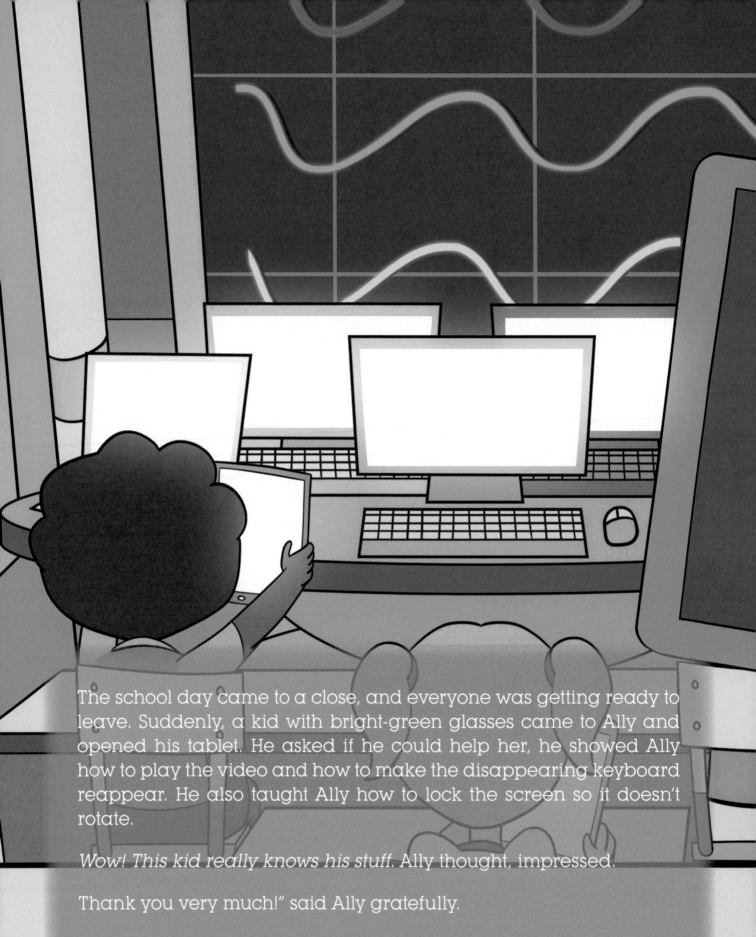

The school day came to a close, and everyone was getting ready to leave. Suddenly, a kid with bright-green glasses came to Ally and opened his tablet. He asked if he could help her, he showed Ally how to play the video and how to make the disappearing keyboard reappear. He also taught Ally how to lock the screen so it doesn't rotate.

Wow! This kid really knows his stuff. Ally thought, impressed.

Thank you very much!" said Ally gratefully.

Ally really appreciated all his help because all this technology was so overwhelming and new to her.

The kid smiled brightly with his green glasses and said,

"No problem, Mrs. AppleBottom!

I'm always here to help. After all, you know, students can help teachers too!", the student said kindly.

Mrs. AppleBottom nodded in appreciation.

Mr. Time-Bot was standing in the doorway observing, and he flashed a gigantic smile and said, "We are all here to help, Mrs. AppleBottom. New things can be difficult to learn, but by embracing the change and staying positive you can always become successful in everything you do."

Mrs. AppleBottom smiled brightly and nodded. She knew that she would persevere!

The classroom transformed into a virtual wonderland as the first rays of the digital dawn broke through creating inspiration.

Educational Technology Week

Name: Mrs. AppleBottom

Mrs. Ally AppleBottom learned a very important lesson that day.

"Mr. Time-Bot, now I know to embrace change with a positive attitude and not be afraid." stated Mrs. AppleBottom with confidence.

"Digital Technology is a big part of our world today, even if it didn't exist when we were children, so I will keep trying my best and learn from my other teacher friends, my students, and of course, from you, Mr. Time-Bot!", Mrs. AppleBottom declared with excitement.

"Superb!" exclaimed Mr. Time-Bot.

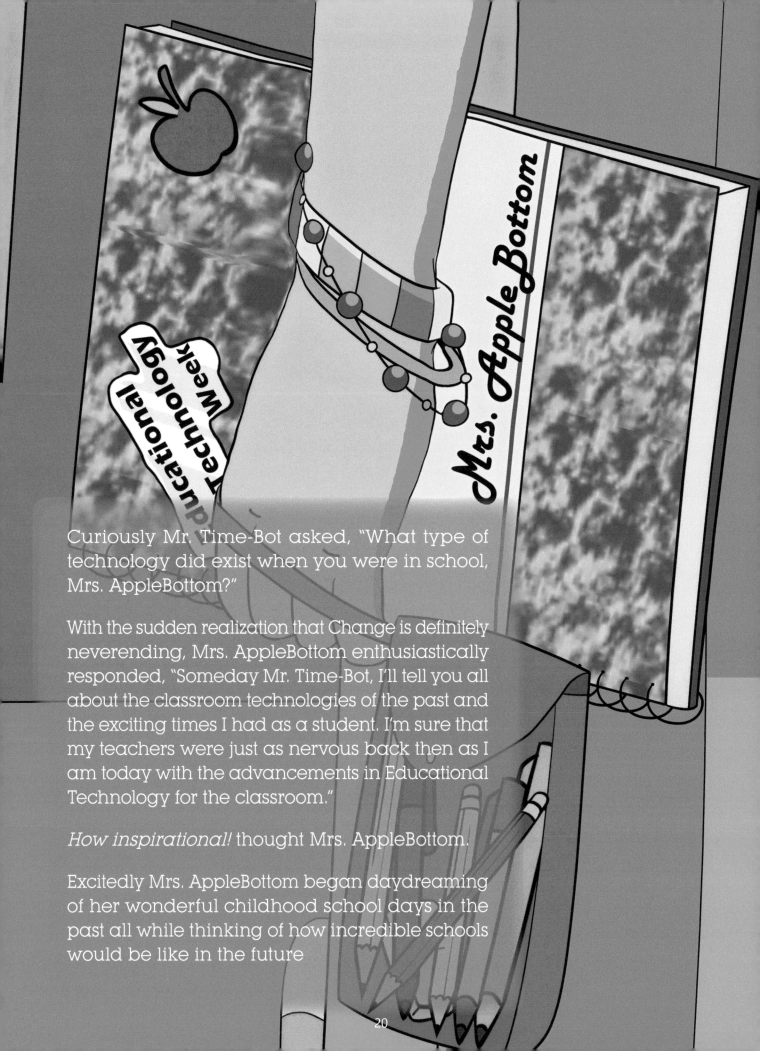

Curiously Mr. Time-Bot asked, "What type of technology did exist when you were in school, Mrs. AppleBottom?"

With the sudden realization that Change is definitely neverending, Mrs. AppleBottom enthusiastically responded, "Someday Mr. Time-Bot, I'll tell you all about the classroom technologies of the past and the exciting times I had as a student. I'm sure that my teachers were just as nervous back then as I am today with the advancements in Educational Technology for the classroom."

How inspirational! thought Mrs. AppleBottom.

Excitedly Mrs. AppleBottom began daydreaming of her wonderful childhood school days in the past all while thinking of how incredible schools would be like in the future

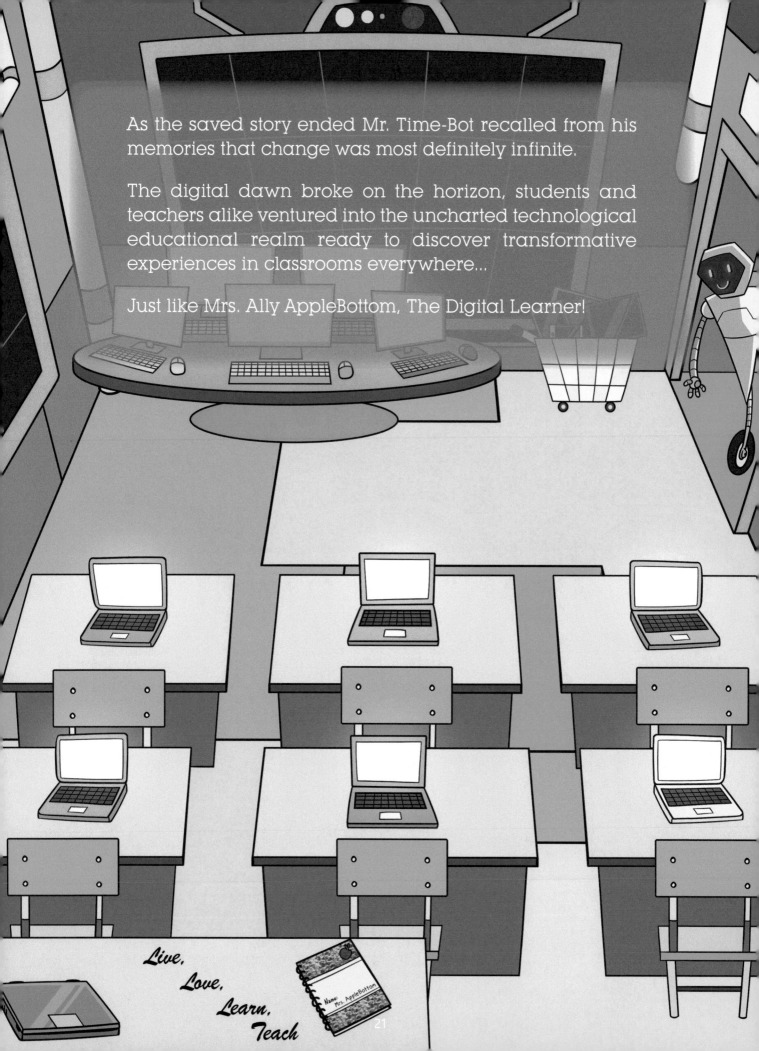

As the saved story ended Mr. Time-Bot recalled from his memories that change was most definitely infinite.

The digital dawn broke on the horizon, students and teachers alike ventured into the uncharted technological educational realm ready to discover transformative experiences in classrooms everywhere...

Just like Mrs. Ally AppleBottom, The Digital Learner!

Live,
Love,
Learn,
Teach

Name:
Mrs. AppleBottom

Educational Technologies:

Past, Present, Future

Past Educational Technologies

Slate and chalk

Radio

Mimeograph

Paper and pencil

Film projector

Tape recorders

Stereoscope

Overhead projector

Television

Present Educational Technologies

Calculator

Educational
digital games

Tablet

Computers

Interactive
whiteboards

Internet

Future Educational Technologies

Virtual reality

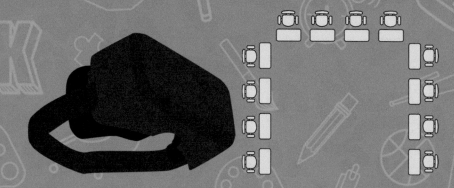

Paperless classroom

School in home community

Augmented reality   Computerized teacher

3D printing

Printed in the United States
by Baker & Taylor Publisher Services